JUMP INTO SPORTS

Ice Skating

By Bob Temple

Ice skaters glide over the ice.
It looks so easy to do!

Ice skating is a fun sport.

In cold weather, outdoor ice **rinks** are great places to skate. Indoor rinks have ice all year long.

Ice rinks have boards around the outside.

An ice skate is a special boot. It has a sharp **blade** on the bottom. There are different types of skates for each type of ice skating.

An ice skater must be able to balance well.

Figure skaters use skates with a **flexible** boot. The blade has a ridge at the front called a **toe pick**. It helps the skater with stops and jumps.

Figure skaters perform to music.

Figure skaters do spins, tricks, and jumps. Judges choose the winners.

Figure skaters wear fancy costumes.

Hockey skates have a stiffer boot. They help the skater speed up and change directions quickly. They also protect the skater's feet.

Hockey skates do not have toe picks.

Hockey players wear lots of **equipment**. They bump and **check** as they try to get the **puck** into the net.

Hockey equipment helps protect the player from getting hurt.

On a **speed skate**, the blade is longer than the boot. The blade has a **hinge**. This allows it to snap away from the boot and back again with each stride.

A speed skater's blades are very thin.

Speed skaters wear helmets and tight suits. They lean forward as they race around an oval track. The fastest racer wins.

Speed skaters also wear gloves or mittens.

Skating is fun no matter which kind you do!

Ice skating takes a lot of practice.

Glossary

blade (BLAYD): The blade is the metal part of an ice skate that glides on the ice. Each type of skating has a specific style of blade.

check (CHEK): In hockey, to check someone is to block them or slow them down. If a check is too rough, a penalty might be called.

equipment (ih-KWIP-munt): Equipment are the things used to play a sport. Hockey players wear equipment to protect themselves.

figure skaters (FIG-yur SKAY-turz): Figure skaters are athletes who perform spins, jumps, and other moves on the ice. Figure skaters are graceful and must have good balance.

flexible (FLEK-suh-bull): To be flexible is to be able to bend. A figure skating boot must be flexible.

hinge (HINJ): A hinge is a joint that holds two things together. Speed skates have a hinge that holds the blade to the boot.

puck (PUHK): A puck is a round rubber disk used in hockey. A hockey player tries to get the puck into the other team's net.

rinks (RINGKZ): Rinks are places where skaters can practice. People can ice skate on indoor rinks all year long.

speed skate (SPEED SKAYT): A speed skate is a type of skate with a long blade. A speed skate is made to help the skater skate very fast.

toe pick (TOE PIK): A toe pick is the notched front part of a figure skate blade. The toe pick helps the figure skater dig into the ice to perform jumps.

To Find Out More

Books

Farbs, C. *Olympic Ice Skating*. New York: Rosen, 2007.

Marsico, Katie, and Cecilia Minden. *Speed Skating*. Ann Arbor, MI: Cherry Lake Publishers, 2008.

Rossiter, Sean, and Paul Carson. *Hockey the NHL Way: The Basics.* Vancouver, British Columbia: Greystone Books, 2006.

Samuels, Rikki. *Kids' Book of Figure Skating: Skills, Strategies, and Techniques*. New York: Citadel, 2004.

Web Sites

Visit our Web site for links about ice skating: *childsworld.com/links*

Note to Parents, Teachers, and Librarians: We routinely verify our Web links to make sure they are safe and active sites. So encourage your readers to check them out!

Index

About the Author

In his long writing career, **Bob Temple** has been a sportswriter and an award-winning author. He has written dozens of books for young readers. Bob owns a development house that specializes in creating children's educational books. He lives with his family in Minnesota.

On the cover: When it is cold, people can skate on frozen lakes and ponds.

Published by The Child's World®
1980 Lookout Drive • Mankato, MN 56003-1705
800-599-READ • www.childsworld.com

ACKNOWLEDGMENTS
The Child's World®: Mary Berendes, Publishing Director
The Design Lab: Design and production
Red Line Editorial: Editorial direction

PHOTO CREDITS: Nicole Waring/iStockphoto, cover; Rich Legg/iStockphoto, cover; Maridav/Shutterstock Images, 3; Carmen Martínez Banús/iStockphoto, 5; PhotoDisc, 6, 14; Joy Brown/Shutterstock Images, 7; Olga Besnard/Shutterstock Images, 9, 11; iofoto/Shutterstock Images, 13; Ryan Kelly/iStockphoto, 15; Jonathan Larsen/Shutterstock Images, 17, 19; Jody Dingle/Shutterstock Images, 21

Printed in the United States of America in Mankato, Minnesota.
November 2009
F11460

LIBRARY OF CONGRESS CATALOGING-IN-PUBLICATION DATA
Temple, Bob.
  Ice skating / by Bob Temple.
     p. cm. — (Jump into sports)
  Includes bibliographical references and index.
  ISBN 978-1-60253-371-4 (library bound : alk. paper)
  1. Skating—Juvenile literature. I. Title. II. Series.
  GV850.223.T46 2009
  796.91—dc22   2009030729

All sports carry a certain amount of risk. To reduce the risk of injury while ice skating, play at your own level, wear all safety gear, and use care and common sense. Never skate on a frozen pond or lake without an adult's permission! The publisher and author take no responsibility or liability for injuries resulting from ice skating.